Yellow

poems by

Janet Joyner

Finishing Line Press
Georgetown, Kentucky

Yellow

Copyright © 2018 by Janet Joyner
ISBN 978-1-63534-791-3 First Edition
All rights reserved under International and Pan-American Copyright Conventions. No part of this book may be reproduced in any manner whatsoever without written permission from the publisher, except in the case of brief quotations embodied in critical articles and reviews.

ACKNOWLEDGMENTS

Greatful acknowledgment is made to the editors of the following publications in which these poems, or earlier versions of them, have appeared:

Camel City Dispatch: "Polishing Magnolia Leaves."
Cold Mountain Review: "Upgivenhetssyndrome"
Forage Journal: "Remains in the Rift."
Poetry South: " Twenty-nine Notches," "The Footstool."
Second Spring 2016 Anthology: " Fire and Ice." Winner of the Superior Literary Achievement Award.
Second Spring 2017 Anthology: "Holly Berries." Winner of the Poetry Award.
The Matador Review: "In Yellow Clover."

Publisher: Leah Maines
Editor: Christen Kincaid
Cover Art: Ellen E. Henson
Author Photo: Ellen E. Henson
Cover Design: Leah Huete

Printed in the USA on acid-free paper.
Order online: www.finishinglinepress.com
also available on amazon.com

Author inquiries and mail orders:
Finishing Line Press
P. O. Box 1626
Georgetown, Kentucky 40324
U. S. A.

Table of Contents

Yellow Bulk 1

Coneflower 2

Upgivenhetssyndrome 3

Ollie and Lil 4

Remains in the Rift 5

The Dying Coyote 6

Twenty-Nine Notches 7

Bearded Iris 8

The Dry Season 9

True Color 10

The Footstool 11

Ötzi The Iceman 12

Cherry Blossoms 13

The Venus Flytrap 14

Fire and Ice 15

Shaping 16

Polishing Magnolia Leaves 17

Holly Berries 18

In Yellow Clover 19

Luminous Yellow 20

For all my blondes...
the little gold finches and those worker bees
with pollen-puffed knees

Yellow Bulk

The hulk of the yellow bulk of her
in those citrus colored Capris
emerging legs first from the Nissan
sports 370 Z, like pupa claspers struggling
to shed tight skin, ill-prepared us for
the sight of those size-ten, wooden, wedged,
open-toed, fuck-me pumps she flung
to the dirt, stuffed her feet inside,
and in them stood, then strode right past us.

Coneflower

Coneflower beauty
is all about eye   and
the yellow stigma
of that bulbous disk
tumescent atop the droopy
petal rays that ring it
like a skimpy skirt
quickly bedraggled
long before the bees
come buzzing
reminding me
of the scant
oft dropped one
above the knees
of that poor mulatto
girl with the diseased
and bulging eyes
who disappeared
from sight before
middle school
was even
half done.

Upgivenhetssyndrome

Thirteen-year-old Georgi,
in his boxers and athletic
socks, lies mute and senseless
on his bed in Garpenberg,
one hundred and twenty miles
northwest of Stockholm.
Like Snow White, Georgi
has fallen away from this world.
The condition he now exhibits
is showing up in emergency rooms
filled with teen-age, Syrian refugees
whose asylum status has expired.
Georgi, for his part, would rather
lie down and die. The Swedes
now even have
a word
for it.

Ollie and Lil

On these windblown sands
and no where else on earth does
the Coachella Valley Milk Vetch
grow. My lover had taken me
there in search of the little purple
flowers that turn blue, blue like
the blue of her eyes, but only after
the bees have done their work. We
would have missed it but for the elderly
couple we encountered by a large
patch of Filaree. Ollie was down
on his knees in the dust and Lil on
her belly, intent with her camera.
Ollie couldn't understand why
the inflorescence was blue. He
did recognize it as Vetch, or looking
like Vetch, he said to her. Ollie, in that
old Dodgers cap, with his eyes sparkling,
still smitten with the white-haired Lil.
He says they're really bird watchers,
but that the two (birds and wild flowers)
sort of go together, and that each year
they cross to Mexico to watch the birds
but end up here in flowers.

Remains in the Rift

After the tsunami took his wife, Takamatsu took
up deep sea diving to try and find her. In a few years
       he had learned that the bodies of drowned people
are usually found poised with buttocks high,
hands and feet dangling. The corpses of scuba divers
       are more like dead bugs, on their backs,
hands and feet floating. He keeps diving, he says, because
it's where he feels closest to her. Heidegger called this type
       of pain a metaphoric rift that holds together things
that have been torn apart. A rift to create a new space
that keeps the connection.

What will perish when I perish
       is the image
of her standing at our kitchen counter, in front of the sink,
hip almost as high as the line
       where the back of her elbow breaks
in the handling of sudsy dishes. It's where
we had most of our arguments,
       after replenishment
refueling with the meal usually I'd been the one to cook.
What remains in our rift, our decades of drift, is the look
       of her haunch poised
in its reveal of that long, smooth curve of her thigh
as the right arm dangles a hand, robotically, towards the next dish.

The Dying Coyote

In the high desert hills
I came upon a still coyote.
His static presence
startled, fixed me there,
freezing my leaking fear
into his nostrils and onto
the buds of my tongue.
He seemed ill, or wounded,
but lay stretched out, head
up, paws out front, like a Sphinx
on guard, doing dog duty.
He hooked me by the eye, held me
there, in those filmy, deep-time eyes
that seemed to know what the rocks
know, to want to signal, to say
if Death *were* come for him,
he would sit right there and calmly
wait for the thing to come to pass.
As if he had this knowledge
in a way that he had always had it,
and in a way that I did not—
making him the greater riddle,
and my passage less secure.

Twenty-Nine Notches

Twenty-nine notches carved
on the Lebombo baboon's
fibula evidence a tool,
a possible mathematical rule.
Or at least a lunar calendar,
millennia senior by far
than the markings honed
on that Ishango bone.
A past when predictions
of the god-swallowing eclipse,
strategically shrewd as politics,
might have been useful,
perhaps even crucial
for those anxious over who shall
remain priestly. Or maybe it was
was always and only menstrual.
The counting sensually consensual
in the accounting for it.
At the dawn of numbers,
one small black woman
on a vast black
continent in the black
of the night,
needing to
get it right.

Bearded Iris
*After Sappho's Fragment 31
rendered by Margaret Reynolds.*

*Every time I look at you.
Every time.
Every time I look.
Every time.*

The red muscle's iamb
quickens

thumps at tympanum's
drum

melting upright bones
and gravity of speech.

Every time.

The fall of your bluish tongue
with its golden beard

spills from stigmatic lip
trussed up in standards

like dew-wet pudendum
shielding gametes

in their leap
to the compatible pistil.

And nothing else is.

Every time.

The Dry Season

In the dry season, the Colorado's water
no longer reaches the Sea of Cortez,
does not go those last seventy miles
over grains and pebbles eroded from
the soaring Rockies by six million years
of water. Now, wherever it is summer,
not one of the great rivers makes it back.

Surely their gods have noticed. No Naiads
come to dance on dead deltas, dried-up
mud-flats. And in the Susquehanna,
male fish have been showing up in drag.
Small mouth bass and little suckers
with eggs in their testes, awash
in endocrine-altering chemicals.

True Color

Yellow is not quite
the natural
color
of my true love's
hair,

nor, of her love,
is true
any more
naturally
the hue.

The Footstool

By the time I came to sit upon it, the stool
        had long ago been painted white
and since acquired that chipped and graying
effect from shoes, though my first memory

of the squat little seat—a flat wooden square,
        its edges wrapped in wicker that arched,
like Victorian gingerbread, down four fat legs
to accrete its miniature elephantine feet—

is not so much of stool, but of tomato,
        a whole, first, fresh-peeled tomato just handed to me; the sweet,
acrid, shocking taste of it, juice dripping from hand, mouth and chin
onto my bare chest and stomach, running all the way down

to the one exception to my nakedness, to the diapers swaddling
        my bottom there on that stubby bench, legs and feet dangling,
dangling before a tin tub filling with the red work of women
singing at their knives and tomatoes.

Red tomato. White stool.
        Where it all begins.

Ötzi The Iceman
for Baltimore, Ferguson, Charlotte...and us all

He bled out more slowly than the ice moved to cover him on the east ridge of the Fineilspitze where the arrow caught him thousands of years ago, long before those stones we call menhirs were fashioned into the mystery of Stonehenge, or Newgrange. So about this naturally mummified man we actually know quite a bit. That his intestinal contents, for instance, showed two meals consumed about eight hours before his death. Analysis of the stomach's remains revealed partially digested Ibex meat, suggesting that he'd had a third meal less than two hours before he died. High levels of copper particles and arsenic were found in his hair, feeding speculation that Ötzi was involved in copper smelting, perhaps even of the axe with its yew handle found at his side, along with a quiver that held, in addition to a bow string and one unfinished yew bow, a total of 14 arrow shafts fashioned from viburnum and dogwood. Two of them were broken, but tipped with flint. The other 12 were unfinished, untipped. There were two birch bark baskets. One held berries and mushrooms deemed to be medicinal; in the other, a type of tinder fungus and what appeared to be a complex fire-lighting kit. His clothes were sophisticated, too. Bearskin cap with chin-strap; cloak of woven grass; and coat, belt, leggings and loin cloth, all made of leather from different skins. The shoes were waterproof, intricate, and seemingly designed for walking in the snow. Evidence, some say, of specialized labor. Cobblers making shoes for other people. One kind of sophistication for builders, one for cobblers, one for shepherds. In the Tyrolean alps, not too far from where Ötzi met his end, there lies a prehistoric stele. One of its base stones depicts an archer poised to fire an arrow toward the back of an unarmed man who is running away. Receding glaciers revealing the true pace of evolution.

Cherry Blossoms

White blooms soon lose
their hour to green,
petals, everywhere
falling,
preface to leaves,
the very ones
that will make
their own way
down, to lie
in these old
ruts, clinging
to our feet
with the drift
of things
unrequited.

The Venus Flytrap

today is a highly evolved apparatus,
snapping shut only when stimulated
by a prey of sufficient status

to trigger the properly acidulated
closure. Too small was simply not worth
the cost, the price of fluids articulated

in digestion of insects whose girth
hardly justified such expenditure.
So, in time, nature naturally gave birth

to a lesser form of discomfiture
for the carnavore, if not the terrestrial bug
whose extracted nutrients, as divestiture,

held ampler advantage for the *snap* over
the *sticky* in design of entrapment devices.
As for dissolving the soft, inner parts, moreover,

with Venus, invariably, the best advice is
avoidance, no matter what the price is.

Fire and Ice
> *apologies to Robert Frost*

I love the way fire begat ice,
and the ice runs home,

the way seed begat flower,
and then stretches on;

love mouth, breast, moon, earth,
things round and curvy,

cycles and orbits, the way
atoms go on, go swervey

at this business
of becoming.

Shaping

Sometimes I see
on the closet floor
my own leather
pumps holding
the shape of my
mother's feet.
It always startles me.
"What is she doing
here?" I think.
But of course
she's been dead
these forty years. And
for the longest time
I thought her feet
were all I had of her.

Polishing Magnolia Leaves

Polishing magnolia leaves
for the funeral wreath
was one way
of laureling her excellence,
as we stood there, side
by side, wiping each leaf
with rags smelling like
memories of man-sweat
and honey-colored beeswax
out of that old rusty can
of Johnson's floor paste
he'd used to gloss, annually,
the college's Main Hall floors;
he, with his dark hands
shining like the mahogany
of her casket, and I, with my white
ones that had taken notes from
her lectures on Cicero and Virgil,
as we did this honor
and grieving,
alone together,
hands waxing.

Holly Berries

This year berries the color of blood
feed no waxwings, spread no seed
to cycle evergreens. My hollies hang
still and heavy with their red weight.
I miss the birds, their hissy whistle,
flutter of wings whirring over the
rudder of that gold-tipped tail,
making the whole tree throb, and me

to question if there's some new
thing birds know first, some
prescience in the beating heart,
like grandmothers on the night
before Antietam or Normandy's
Omaha Beach; to wonder, somehow,
now we've determined to be *great again,*
if throngs of dead women

aren't hovering about in cahoots
with birds boycotting holly berries;
clouds of them, full of the dead, like covies
of little red hens, wanting to attract
attention, wave flags, spell warnings,
parlay a stay of decay,
if flow reverses how to go
and mushrooms grow in the sky.

In Yellow Clover

> *...That so our hearts might reach*
> *And touch within the yellow clover,*
> *Love's letter to be glad about*
> *Like sunshine when it came!...*
> —Yellow Clover, A Book of Remembrance
> Katharine Lee Bates, 1859-1929
> for
> Katharine Coman, 1857-1915)

That such a one was not undone
by a home costumed as house,
as merely abode within the code
defining legitimate spouse,
would have been helpful
to know as we tried to grow,
puffed out like fledglings
on the edge of our school room
nests, belting out song
and full-throated belief
in her purpled mountains
and plains of fruit—new recruits
to the double song hailing a land
that promised to span any
discouraging word that might
someday be *heard* on this
home on the range grand enough
for *Solomon Levi*, his shops of rough
cloth, and that *Spanish Cavalier*
playing *on his guitar, a tune dear...*
so near to, and all at once,
de camp town races
sing dis song...
O-doo-da-day—

before we learned
of the *autos-da-fé*.

Luminous Yellow

Eye catching color
of sunflower
and daffodil,
of egg yolks
and butter,
canaries and bees
happy faces,
post-its,
and the Tour de France
jersey,
of happiness, sunshine
and spring—
except when
it signals
caution,
cowardice,
or jaundice,
pestilence,
or malaria,
and whose source pigments,
as any painter
can attest,
are all toxic metals.

Janet Joyner was born and grew up in Marion, South Carolina, a town that sits in a region of midland and coastal plains crisscrossed by rivers and streams whose names—Waccamaw, Pee Dee, Santee, Withlacoochee, Congaree—not only echo those of the native tribes who once lived by their banks, but also form the first auditory medium that schools a child's ear to a place, and to the world. Likewise the work songs of an era when harvesting was still done by hand, when the "cropping and grading" of tobacco on her family's farms was largely done by Gullah or Geechee women whose rhythms and rich vowels left their mark.

Professor of French Language and Literature at the University of North Carolina School of the Arts until her retirement in 1994, Joyner is the winner of the Poetry Society of South Carolina's 2010 Dubose and Dorothy Heyward Poetry Prize. Her poems have won distinctions in *Bay Leaves* of the North Carolina Poetry Council, and *Flying South '14*, the Superior Literary Award for *Second Spring 2016 Anthology*, and the Poetry Award for *Second Spring 2017 Anthology*; her poem "Holly Berries" was long-listed for the 2017 *Rialto* prize; her "Twenty-nine Notches" was a semi-finalist for the United Kingdom's 2016 Bridport Prize, as well as a finalist for the 2016 Poets Billow Prize. Her "Cicadas Thrumming" was anthologized in *The Southern Poetry Anthology: volume vii: North Carolina*, 2015. Her short stories have appeared in *The Crescent Review* and *Flying South*. She is the translator of *Le Dieu désarmé*, by Luc-François Dumas. This is her second collection of poems.

www.ingramcontent.com/pod-product-compliance
Lightning Source LLC
LaVergne TN
LVHW041525070426
835507LV00013B/1820